Introduction

The type and varieties of pasta available are enormous but here we show you a small selection.

For general purposes, the fourteen or so varieties listed in the book should be adequate for most culinary purposes.

This edition published 1994 by Merehurst Limited

Ferry House, 51-57 Lacy Road, Putney, London SW15 1PR

Reprinted 1994, 1997

Copyright © Gräfe und Unzer GmbH 1992, Munich

ISBN 1 874567 27 1

All : = 1
Foll an no

Eggs used are a medium size 3 unless otherwise stated.

For additional hints and tips on cooking pasta, skinning tomatoes, chopping herbs and making your own pasta, see pages 18-19 and 34-35.

Kilojoules and kilocalories at the end of each recipe are represented by the letters kj and kcal.

Designed by Clive Dorman & Co.
Printed in Italy by G. Canale & C.S.p.A

Distributed in the UK by J.B. Fairfax Press Limited, 9 Trinity Centre, Park Farm, Wellingborough, Northants NN8 6ZB

Distributed in Australia by J.B. Fairfax Press Pty Ltd, 80 McLachlan Avenue, Rushcutters Bay, Sydney, NSW 2011

Written By Annette Wolter

Spaghetti alla Carbonara

Serves 4

A classic combination of spaghetti with cream, bacon and cheese.

Preparation time: about 15 minutes
Cooking time: about 15 minutes

2 litres (3½ pints/8 cups) boiling water
1½ teaspoons salt
2 tablespoons olive oil, plus 1 teaspoon
375g (12oz) spaghetti
125g (4oz) streaky bacon, rinds removed
45g (1½oz) Pecorino or Parmesan cheese
2 cloves garlic
3 eggs
4 tablespoons whipping cream
Salt and pepper to taste

1 Have ready a warm serving dish, keeping it in a low oven until the spaghetti is ready.

2 Pour boiling water into a large saucepan. Add salt and 1 teaspoon oil. Bring to the boil. Ease in spaghetti without breaking. As it softens, it will yield to gentle pressure and settle in a coil in the base of pan. Stir well to separate.

3 Cook pasta, uncovered, for 7-10 minutes, until spaghetti is 'al dente' or just tender to the bite. Leave to stand for 1 minute.

4 Meanwhile chop bacon coarsely. Grate cheese. Peel garlic and cut each lengthwise into 4 strips.

5 Heat remaining oil in a second large saucepan. Add garlic and fry gently until golden brown. Remove pan from heat.

6 Tip bacon into the saucepan and stir-fry briskly until crisp and golden. Take pan off the heat, leaving bacon where it is.

7 Thoroughly drain spaghetti, and add to pan of oil and bacon.

8 Beat eggs, cream and cheese together. Season to taste with salt and pepper and pour over the spaghetti. Return pan to moderate heat.

9 Cook and toss gently with 2 spoons until egg mixture thickens slightly and clings to the spaghetti. Do not over heat or the mixture will scramble.

10 Transfer pasta to the warm serving dish and eat straight away. A simple green salad goes well with the richness of this dish.

Nutritional value per portion:
about 3100kj/740kcal
Protein: 25g
Fat: 39g
Carbohydrate: 73g

Spaghetti alla Carbonara

Fettucine with Bacon and Cheese

Serves 4

Flat pasta ribbons with bacon and peas makes a perfect midweek supper.

Preparation time: about 10 minutes
Cooking time: about 15 minutes

125g (4oz) streaky bacon, rinds removed
2 litres (3½ pints/8 cups) boiling water
1½ teaspoons salt
1 tablespoon olive oil, plus 1 teaspoon
375g (12oz) wide fettucine
155ml (5fl oz/1⅔ cup) whipping cream
315g (10oz) frozen peas

1 Cut bacon into narrow strips, removing any small pieces of white bone.

2 Pour boiling water into a large saucepan. Add salt and 1 teaspoon oil and bring back to the boil. Lower in the fettucine and stir well to separate.

3 Cook pasta, uncovered for 7-10 minutes or until 'al dente' or just tender to the bite. Leave to stand for 1 minute.

4 Meanwhile, heat remaining tablespoon of olive oil separately in a large pan until sizzling. Add bacon and fry over a moderate heat until crisp and golden brown, stirring occasionally.

5 Mix in cream and peas, cover and simmer for 3-4 minutes, stirring occasionally.

6 Drain fettucine, add to pan of bacon mixture and toss with 2 spoons over low heat until piping hot.

7 Transfer to a warm serving dish and accompany with grilled or fried tomatoes.

½ amount of pasta
2 " of cream
½ " of peas

Nutritional value per portion:
about 3000kj/710kcal
Protein: 21g
Fat: 33g
Carbohydrate: 82g

Fettucine with Bacon and Cheese

Spaghetti Bolognese

Serves 4

An internationally-famed classic from Bologna, in Northern Italy.

Preparation time: 20 minutes
Cooking time: about 1 hour

60g (2oz) piece of Parmesan cheese
1 medium onion
1 medium carrot
2 sticks celery
2 beef tomatoes
45g (1½oz) butter
1 tablespoon tomato purée (paste)
500g (1lb) lean minced beef
155ml (¼ pint/⅔ cup) meat stock
1 clove
1 medium dried bay leaf
Salt and pepper to taste
2 litres (3½ pints/8 cups) boiling water
1½ teaspoons salt
1 teaspoon olive oil
375g (12oz) spaghetti
155ml (¼ pint/⅔ cup) red wine

1 Grate cheese and put into a small serving bowl. Set aside.

2 Peel and chop onion and carrot or coarsely grate. Cut celery into thin, diagonal strips. Skin tomatoes (see step-by-step instructions on page 18-19) and chop.

3 Melt butter in a saucepan until sizzling. Add the onion, carrot and celery and fry for about 5 minutes until light golden brown.

4 Stir in chopped tomatoes, tomato purée (paste) and the minced beef. Stir-fry with a fork for about 10 minutes until meat looks brown and crumbly. Keep heat fairly brisk.

5 Pour in meat stock then add clove, bay leaf and seasoning. Bring to the boil, lower heat and cover. Simmer for 45 minutes, stirring occasionally.

6 To cook spaghetti, pour boiling water into a large saucepan. Add salt and oil. Bring back to the boil. Ease in spaghetti without breaking. As it softens, it will yield to gentle pressure and settle in a coil in the base of the pan. Stir well to separate.

7 Cook pasta, uncovered, for 7-10 minutes until 'al dente' or just tender to the bite. Leave to stand for 1 minute.

8 Meanwhile, add red wine to meat sauce and season with salt and pepper. Leave uncovered and simmer until spaghetti is ready.

9 Drain spaghetti thoroughly. Divide equally between 4 warm plates and top with sauce. Accompany with the Parmesan cheese.

Nutritional value per portion:
about 3300kj/790kcal
Protein: 40g
Fat: 31g
Carbohydrate: 78g

Spaghetti Bolognese

Fettucine with Tuna Sauce

Serves 4

This supper dish is quick and easy to make using storecupboard ingredients.

Preparation time: about 15 minutes
Cooking time: about 40 minutes

2 cloves garlic
220g (7oz) can tuna in oil
440g (14oz) can tomatoes
15g (½oz) fresh parsley
1 tablespoon olive oil, plus 1 teaspoon
1½ teaspoons salt
2 litres (3½ pints/8 cups) water
375g (12oz) wide fettucine
Fresh basil leaves for garnishing

1 Peel garlic and finely chop. Take tuna out of can, reserving oil, flake fish into large chunks. Chop tomatoes. Chop parsley fairly finely, removing stalks.

2 Pour 1 tablepoon olive oil and oil from can of tuna into a medium saucepan. Add garlic and fry until pale gold.

3 Add the tomatoes and ½ teaspoon salt then cover and simmer gently for 20 minutes. Add tuna and parsley and continue to simmer for 10 minutes while cooking pasta.

4 Pour boiling water into a large saucepan. Add remaining teaspoon salt and remaining teaspoon oil and bring back to the boil. Lower in the fettucine. Stir well to separate.

5 Cook pasta, uncovered for 7-10 minutes until 'al dente' or just tender to the bite. Leave to stand for 1 minute. Drain and transfer to 4 warm plates. Spoon over tuna sauce and garnish with basil.

Nutritional value per portion:
about 2700kj/640kcal
Protein: 32g
Fat: 23g
Carbohydrate: 77g

Fettucine with Tuna Sauce

Wholemeal Macaroni with Mushroom Sauce

Serves 4

Mushrooms in cream make a wonderful sauce for wholemeal pasta

Preparation time: about 15 minutes
Cooking time: about 20 minutes

1 medium onion
2 cloves garlic
315g (10oz) button mushrooms
1 tablespoon olive oil, plus 1 teaspoon
315ml (½ pint/1¼ cups) vegetable stock
2 litres (3½ pints/8 cups) boiling water
1½ teaspoons salt
375g (12oz) wholemeal elbow macaroni
2 tablespoons fruity white wine or
    1 teaspoon lemon juice
2 pinches dried herbs
6 tablespoons soured cream
1 egg yolk
2 tablespoons snipped fresh chives

1 Peel onion and garlic and chop both finely. Trim and rinse mushrooms and cut into slender slices.

2 Heat 1 tablespoon oil in a medium saucepan. Add onion and garlic and fry fairly gently until pale golden. Stir in mushrooms and fry for 2 minutes.

3 Add stock to pan, bring to boil and cover. Simmer gently for 10 minutes.

4 Pour boiling water into a large saucepan. Add salt and remaining teaspoon oil and bring back to the boil. Tip in the macaroni then stir well to separate.

5 Cook pasta, uncovered for 6-9 minutes until 'al dente' or just tender to the bite. Stand for 1 minute.

6 Meanwhile, finish the sauce. Purée the mushroom mixture in a blender or food processor. Pour back into saucepan.

7 Add the wine or lemon juice and herb salt. Whisk cream and egg yolk together. Pour into pan. Reheat, stirring, without boiling or egg might curdle.

8 Drain macaroni and tip into a warm serving dish. Spoon over the mushroom sauce, then sprinkle with chives.

Nutritional value per portion:
about 1900kj/450kcal
Protein: 19g
Fat: 10g
Carbohydrate: 70g

Wholemeal Macaroni with Mushroom Sauce

Spaghetti alla Napoletana

Serves 4

This delicious fresh tasting basil and tomato sauce makes a perfect accompaniment to Spaghetti.

Preparation time: about 15 minutes
Cooking time: about 25 minutes

1 large onion
15g (½oz) fresh parsley
8 leaves fresh basil
4 tablespoons olive oil, plus 1 teaspoon
2 x 440g (14oz) cans tomatoes
½ teaspoon ground paprika
1 teaspoon granulated sugar
2½ teaspoons salt
2 litres (3½ pints/8 cups) boiling water
375g (12oz) spaghetti
45g (1½oz) grated Pecorino or Parmesan cheese

1 Peel and finely chop onion. Chop parsley finely, removing stalks. Chop basil leaves.

2 For sauce, pour 4 tablespoons oil into a medium saucepan, heat until sizzling then add onion. Fry gently until light golden brown.

3 Add parsley and basil to saucepan with tomatoes. Cook tomatoes until hot, crushing them against sides of pan with a wooden spoon.

4 Add paprika, sugar and 1 teaspoon salt. Bring to boil, lower heat and cover. Simmer gently for 10 minutes, stirring fairly frequently.

5 Pour boiling water into a large saucepan. Add remaining 1½ teaspoons salt and 1 teaspoon oil. Bring back to the boil. Ease in spaghetti without breaking. As it softens, it will yield to gentle pressure and settle in a coil in the base of pan. Stir well to separate.

6 Cook pasta, uncovered, for 7-10 minutes until spaghetti is 'al dente' or just tender to the bite. Leave to stand for 1 minute. Drain thoroughly and transfer equal amounts to 4 warm plates.

7 Spoon sauce over spaghetti and pass cheese separately.

Nutritional value per portion:
about 2400kj/570kcal
Protein: 20g
Fat: 18g
Carbohydrate: 83g

Spaghetti alla Napoletana

Spinach Fettucine with Cheese Sauce

Serves 4

This creamy cheese sauce is quick and easy to prepare and marries well with all types of pasta.

Preparation time: about 10 minutes
Cooking time: about 10 minutes

2 litres (3½ pints/8 cups) boiling water
1 teaspoon salt
1½ teaspoons olive oil
375g (12oz) green fettucine
315ml (½ pint/1¼ cups) vegetable stock
220g (7oz) French Boursin cheese, with or without herbs
2 teaspoons cornflour
2 tablespoons white wine
Salt and pepper to taste

1 Pour boiling water into a large saucepan. Add salt and oil. Bring back to the boil. Lower in the fettucine and stir well to separate.

2 Cook pasta, uncovered for 7-10 minutes until fettucine is 'al dente' or just tender to the bite. Leave to stand for 1 minute.

3 Heat the vegetable stock until it just comes up to the boil. Put the cheese into a bowl and mash finely with a fork. Gradually blend in stock.

4 Return to saucepan. Mix cornflour with wine until smooth. Add to the cheese and stock mixture.

5 Slowly bring to the boil, stirring continuously. Simmer for 1 minute, then season. Remove from heat and cover.

6 Drain fettucine thoroughly. Transfer to 4 warm plates and spoon over sauce.

Nutritional value per portion:
about 2000kj/480kcal
Protein: 15g
Fat: 19g
Carbohydrate: 56g

16

Spinach Fettucine with Cheese Sauce

Step-by step

COOKING PASTA

1 'Al dente' means with a bit of bite and is used to describe pasta which is cooked just long enough to swell yet remain firm in texture. To cook 'al dente', tip the pasta into boiling, salted water and stir.

2 Ease long spaghetti into boiling water without breaking. As it softens, it will yield to gentle pressure and settle itself down in the base of the pan. Stir well to separate.

3 Cook pasta, uncovered, for 7-12 minutes (depending on size) until pasta has reached the 'al dente' stage, tasting it once or twice as it nears the end of its cooking time. Stand for 1 minute, then drain and serve.

SKINNING TOMATOES

4 Cut a cross on the base of each tomato. Lower into a pan of gently boiling water and switch off heat. Leave for 1 minute.

5 Rinse tomatoes under cold water then peel off skin with the help of a small knife.

6 Cut out the hard white core and cut up tomatoes as instructed in the recipe.

CHOPPING HERBS

7 Wash herbs. Leave until well drained or pat dry with absorbent kitchen paper.

8 Pull leaves away from stalks and put on to a chopping board.

9 Chop herbs finely with a sharp cook's knife or a 2-bladed mezzaluna (see picture 8).

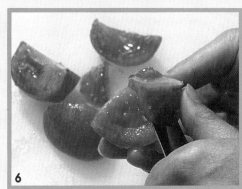

19

Spaghetti al Pesto

Serves 4

Brilliantly-coloured green with basil, this is a simple pasta dish enhanced with now readily-available pesto sold in jars in most supermarket chains and speciality food shops. A recipe for home-made pesto for keen cooks is included here.

Preparation time: about 15 minutes
Cooking time: about 15 minutes

30g (1oz) fresh basil
3 cloves garlic
45g (1½oz) pine nuts
125g (4oz) grated Pecorino or Parmesan Cheese
6 tablespoons olive oil, plus 1 teaspoon
Salt and pepper to taste
2 litres (3½ pints/ 8 cups) boiling water
1½ teaspoons salt
375g (12oz) spaghetti
Sprig of fresh basil for garnishing

1 Chop basil leaves very finely and put into a bowl.

2 Peel garlic and crush on top of basil.

3 Chop pine nuts finely and add to basil and garlic with grated cheese. Gradually beat in 6 tablespoons of the oil.

4 Season to taste with salt and pepper, cover and set aside.

5 Pour water into a large saucepan. Add salt and remaining 1 teaspoon oil. Bring back to the boil. Ease in spaghetti without breaking. As it softens, it will yield to gentle pressure and settle in a coil in the base of the pan. Stir well to separate.

6 Cook pasta, uncovered, for 7-10 minutes until spaghetti is 'al dente' or just tender to the bite. Drain off water, leaving about 2 tablespoons behind in saucepan with the spaghetti.

7 Mix in pesto and toss thoroughly with 2 spoons.

8 Transfer to a warm dish to serve and garnish.

Nutritional value per portion:
about 3600kj/860kcal
Protein: 24g
Fat: 44g
Carbohydrate: 77g

Spaghetti al Pesto

Twistetti with Tomato Sauce

Serves 4

A rustic Mediterranean dish of tomatoes, olives, anchovies and pasta.

Preparation time: about 15 minutes
Cooking time: about 25 minutes

3 cloves garlic
8 canned anchovy fillets, in oil
125g (4oz) black olives, stoned
3 tablespoons olive oil, plus 1 teaspoon
440g (14oz) can chopped tomatoes
1 tablespoon small capers, drained
½ teaspoon paprika
Salt to taste
2 litres (3½ pints/8 cups) boiling water
1½ teaspoons salt
375g (12oz) spiral pasta

1 Peel garlic and crush into a medium saucepan. Chop anchovies fairly finely. Chop olives coarsely. Add both to pan with 3 tablespoons of the olive oil.

2 Fry over moderate heat until garlic turns pale golden. Stir in tomatoes, capers, paprika and salt.

3 Bring to boil, lower heat and cover. Simmer gently for 20 minutes, stirring fairly frequently.

4 After 10 minutes, pour boiling water into a large saucepan. Add salt and remaining oil. Bring back to the boil. Tip in the pasta and stir well to separate.

5 Cook pasta, uncovered, for 6-9 minutes until 'al dente' or just tender to the bite. Stand for 1 minute, then drain and transfer to a warm serving dish.

6 Spoon over sauce and serve straight away.

Nutritional value per portion:
about 2600kj/620kcal
Protein: 19g
Fat: 26g
Carbohydrate: 78g

22

Twistetti with Tomato Sauce

Summer Spaghetti

Serves 4

A delicate, creamy sauce speckled with courgettes (zucchini) and ham.

Preparation time: about 30 minutes
Cooking time: about 20 minutes

625g (1¼lb) courgettes (zucchini)
2 cloves garlic
1 medium onion
1 tablespoon olive oil, plus 1 teaspoon
125g (4oz) gammon
315ml (½ pint/1¼ cup) vegetable stock
Salt and pepper to taste
Pinch of dried oregano
2 litres (3½ pints/8 cups) boiling water
1½ teaspoons salt
375g (12oz) spaghetti
5 tablespoons crème fraîche

1 Top and tail courgettes (zucchini), wash and dry then cut each one lengthwise into narrow strips. Cut strips into small dice.

2 Peel garlic and onion and finely chop both.

3 Heat 1 tablespoon of the oil in a large saucepan until hot and sizzling. Add garlic and onion and fry fairly gently until pale golden.

4 Add courgettes (zucchini) and continue to fry for about 5 minutes. Meanwhile, cut gammon into narrow strips. Add to fried vegetables with stock.

5 Bring to the boil, stirring. Season with salt, pepper and oregano. Lower heat, cover and simmer gently for 10 minutes.

6 Pour boiling water into a second large saucepan. Add salt and remaining teaspoon oil. Bring back to the boil. Ease in spaghetti without breaking. As it softens, it will yield to gentle pressure and settle in a coil in the base of the pan. Stir well to separate.

7 Meanwhile, cook pasta, uncovered, for 7-10 minutes until 'al dente' or just tender to the bite. Leave to stand for 1 minute then thoroughly drain and transfer to a large, warm serving dish.

8 Add crème fraîche to sauce, heat through briefly and pour over spaghetti. Toss with 2 spoons until well-mixed. Serve straight away.

Nutritional value per portion:
about 2000kj/480kcal
Protein: 17g
Fat: 17g
Carbohydrate: 65g

Summer Spaghetti

Spaghetti with Garlic Oil and Herbs

Serves 4

Strongly flavoured with garlic, this is a favourite pasta dish in Southern Italy.

Preparation time: about 25 minutes
Cooking time: about 10 minutes

4 cloves garlic
30g (1oz) fresh parsley
8 fresh basil leaves
6 tablespoons olive oil, plus 1 teaspoon
Salt and pepper to taste
2 litres (3½ pints/8 cups) water
1½ teaspoons salt
375g (12oz) spaghetti

1 Peel garlic and crush directly into a small saucepan. Chop parsley, discarding stalks. Finely chop basil.

2 Add 6 tablespoons of the oil to pan of garlic and fry gently until light golden. Mix in parsley and basil and season well with salt and pepper. Leave over a very low heat.

3 Pour boiling water into a large saucepan. Add salt and remaining teaspoon oil. Bring back to the boil. Ease in spaghetti without breaking. As it softens, it will yield to gentle pressure and settle in a coil in the base of pan. Stir well to separate.

4 Cook pasta, uncovered for 7-10 minutes or until spaghetti is 'al dente' or just tender to the bite. Leave to stand for 1 minute. Drain thoroughly and tip into a warm serving dish.

5 Spoon over the garlic and herb oil and toss with 2 spoons until well mixed.

Nutritional value per portion:
about 2300kj/550kcal
Protein: 14g
Fat: 23g
Carbohydrate: 74g

Spaghetti with Garlic Oil and Herbs

Spaghetti Omelette

Serves 4

Children will love this fun omelette.

Preparation time: about 20 minutes
Cooking time: about 25 minutes

2 litres (3½ pints/3 cups) boiling water
1½ teaspoons salt
1 teaspoon olive oil
375g (12oz) spaghetti
3 eggs
155ml (¼ pint/⅔ cup) whipping cream
125g (4oz) grated Parmesan cheese
Salt and pepper to taste
45g (1½oz) butter
1 tablespoon snipped fresh chives

1 Pour boiling water into a large saucepan. Add salt and oil. Bring back to the boil. Ease in spaghetti without breaking. As it softens, it will yield to gentle pressure and settle in a coil in the base of pan. Stir well to separate.

2 Cook pasta uncovered, for 7-10 minutes until 'al dente' or just tender to the bite. Leave to stand for 1 minute. Thoroughly drain and leave to cool.

3 To complete, beat eggs and cream together. Stir in two-thirds of the cheese and season with salt and pepper.

4 Melt half the butter in a large, non-stick frying pan.

5 Add the spaghetti in an even layer and fry for about 5 minutes over a moderate heat until underside is golden.

6 Pour in the egg mixture then cover pan with a lid. Continue to cook slowly for 5 minutes then uncover.

7 Sprinkle top of omelette with remaining cheese then dot with flakes of remaining butter.

8 Stand pan under a hot grill, making sure handle is away from source of heat and grill for 1-2 minutes or until top is well-browned.

9 Cut omelette into 4 portions with a non-stick spatula, sprinkle with chives and serve straight away.

Nutritional value per portion:
about 3000kj/710kcal
Protein: 28g
Fat: 35g
Carbohydrate: 73g

Spaghetti Omelette

Macaroni with Ham

Serves 4

A variation on macaroni cheese, this dish makes a substantial supper dish served with crusty bread and a mixed salad.

Preparation time: about 15 minutes
Cooking time: about 30 minutes

2 litres (3½ pints/8 cups) boiling water
1½ teaspoons salt
1 teaspoon olive oil
375g (12oz) elbow macaroni
6 tablespoons milk
315g (10oz) frozen peas
315g (10oz) ham
1 medium onion
60g (2oz) Cheddar cheese
15g (½oz) fresh parsley
1 tablespoon corn oil
155ml (¼ pint/⅔ cup) soured cream
2 eggs
Salt and pepper to taste
30g (1oz) butter
Chopped fresh parsley for garnishing

1 Pour boiling water into a large saucepan. Add salt and olive oil. Bring back to the boil. Tip in the macaroni then stir well to separate.

2 Cook pasta, uncovered, for 6-9 minutes until 'al dente' or until just tender to the bite. Stand for 1 minute. Drain.

3 Meanwhile prepare remaining ingredients. Bring milk to boil in a separate pan. Add peas. Cover and cook for 3 minutes.

4 Chop ham coarsely. Peel and finely chop onion. Grate cheese. Chop parsley finely, discarding stalks. Set oven to 200C 400F Gas 6. Butter a fairly shallow ovenproof dish.

5 Heat corn oil in a pan until hot and sizzling. Add ham and onion and fry until pale golden. Drain macaroni thoroughly and mix into fried ingredients with parsley. Spoon into ovenproof dish.

6 Beat cream and eggs together, add peas and milk, and season well with salt and pepper. Pour over macaroni mixture.

7 Sprinkle with cheese then top with flakes of butter.

8 Bake in oven for 20 minutes until golden brown and bubbly. Garnish and serve.

Nutritional value per portion:
about 2900kj/690kcal
Protein: 33g
Fat: 32g
Carbohydrate: 67g

Macaroni with Ham

Buccatini Gratin with Aubergines

Serves 4

A delicious pasta and vegetable dish which can be made all year round.

Preparation time: about 15 minutes
Cooking time: about 35 minutes

3 litres (3½ pints/½ cup) boiling water
1½ teaspoons salt
2 tablespoons olive oil, plus 1 teaspoon
200g (7oz) buccatini
500g (1lb) aubergines (eggplants)
2 medium onions
5 fresh basil leaves
440g (14oz) can tomatoes
Salt and pepper to taste
125g (4oz) grated Gruyère cheese
155ml (¼ pint/1⅔ cups) whipping cream
2 eggs

1 Pour boiling water into a large saucepan. Add salt and 1 teaspoon of the oil. Bring back to the boil. Ease in buccatini without breaking. As it softens, it will yield to gentle pressure and settle in a coil in the base of pan. Stir well to separate.

2 Cook pasta, uncovered for 7-10 minutes until 'al dente' or just tender to the bite. Leave to stand for 1 minute. Drain buccatini and set aside. Set oven to 200C 400F Gas 6.

3 Meanwhile, prepare remaining ingredients. Top and tail aubergines (eggplants) then cut each one into small cubes. Peel and chop onions. Cut basil leaves into strips. Lift tomatoes out of can and coarsely chop.

4 Heat remaining 2 tablespoons of the oil in a large frying pan until sizzling and

hot. Add onions and fry until light golden. Mix in aubergines (eggplants) and continue to fry for 4 minutes.

5 Spoon into a well-greased ovenproof dish then add tomato juice from can and the chopped tomatoes. Season well with salt and pepper then sprinkle with half the cheese. Spread buccatini evenly over the top.

6 Beat cream and eggs together. Season to taste. Pour over buccatini then sprinkle with basil and remaining cheese. Bake in oven, uncovered, for 20-25 minutes until piping hot and golden brown.

Nutritional value per portion:
about 2300kj/550kcal
Protein: 21g
Fat: 29g
Carbohydrate: 50g

Buccatini Gratin with Aubergines

Step-by-step

HOME-MADE PASTA
410g (13oz) strong plain flour
1 teaspoon salt
4 size 4 eggs
cold water for mixing

1 Sift flour and salt in a mound on to work surface and make a fairly large and deep well in the middle. Break in eggs.

2 Using a fork, beat eggs together, at the same time drawing in some of the flour.

3 With both hands, gently toss flour from the outside into the middle over eggs and work ingredients to a crumbly dough.

4 If dough stays on the dry side, work in a little water. Knead to a smooth dough.

5 Continue to knead dough with the heel of your hand for 10-15 minutes. Wrap in a floured tea towel and leave for 15 minutes.

6 Cut dough in half and roll each out thinly on a floured surface.

7 Dust lightly with flour then roll up both outside edges evenly towards the centre. Leave to stand for about 7-8 minutes, covered lightly with a floured cloth.

8 Cut into narrow, medium or wide strips, as you like.

9 Shake out each strip on the cloth until it loosens and unrolls. Cover lightly with a piece of non-stick baking paper and leave pasta to dry out for 20-40 minutes, depending on room temperature and humidity. Cook pasta for 5-6 minutes only in boiling salted water, drain thoroughly and use as required.